STORY SEEDS GRIMOIRE

DISCOVER YOUR NEEDS THROUGH NARRATIVE

LILY ROSE

CONTENTS

Story Seeds Grimoire:

Discover Your Needs Through Narrative

Published by Rose & Raven LLC
www.rose-raven.com

First Edition: 2026

Created with Vellum

For Brian, my living granite.

May this guide you with love on your excavation expedition.

A VOGON WORD BEFORE YOU WANDER IN

This Grimoire is a creative and reflective tool, not a substitute for professional care.

The writing prompts, interpretations, and reflections contained within this book are intended for personal exploration, creative expression, and self-discovery. They are not intended to diagnose, treat, cure, or prevent any mental health condition, medical condition, or psychological disorder.

If you are struggling with mental health concerns, trauma, grief, addiction, suicidal ideation, or any other condition that warrants professional support, please reach out to a licensed mental health professional, physician, or qualified care provider. The work in this book can complement professional support beautifully...but it cannot replace it, and it was never meant to.

The author is not a licensed therapist, counselor, psychologist, or medical professional. She is a writer, astrologer, yoga instructor, and storyteller drawing on decades of personal experience with character creation, narrative work, and self-reflection. She is also a Uranian Scorpio with a Virgo Stellium and Mercury Rx conjunct her Sun. The insights offered here are her own and should be considered as such...perspectives to consider, not prescriptions to follow.

Engaging with these prompts may surface unexpected emotions, memories, or insights. This is normal and often part of the work...but if anything that arises feels overwhelming or unsafe to process alone, please pause and seek appropriate support. Your wellbeing comes first. Always.

By using this book, you acknowledge that you are responsible for your own emotional and mental wellbeing, and that you will seek qualified professional help when needed.

Yadda,

Yadda,

Yadda,

Zing.

❧

THE MAGIC WITHIN

WHY YOUR CHARACTERS KNOW MORE ABOUT YOU THAN YOU DO.

The stories we tell, tell a lot about us...if only we listen.

This is a Story Seed Grimoire, a book of spells, after a fashion. But these spells don't use candles or eye of newt...if I were going to write that I'd call for two eyes anyway...no these spells take the form of story prompts. They work their magic by slipping past your logical, monkey mind and summoning your soul from the depths of your unconscious. This wondrous, creative, guileless part of you has the most amazing things to say.

You see, the characters we create are more than just characters. We breathe parts of ourselves into each one, from the main character, to the villain, to the grocer with a single line of dialogue.

The protective knight you write about might be showing your need to finally be protected yourself.

The pithy rogue with trust issues and a bottomless tankard could be drinking down your fear of betrayal. A cup filled with experiences waiting to be processed.

The wide-eyed healer quick to cast her last cure wounds spell may whisper of a deep desire to receive and be tended to in turn.

I discovered this truth through decades of creating my own plucky adventurers, through telling stories on the page, at the table, and around the fire. Patterns emerged over time, archetypes played over and over again, common themes occurring for years that no longer appeared as I grew, changed, and had certain needs met. The free-roaming elven druid I created decades ago was already walking the life I'm only now stepping into. She knew before I did.

And now we both get to imbue you with a little bit of that magic, through this Grimoire. Use it well, use it as often as you feel called to, and always be kind to yourself. You're doing the best you can in this moment with the tools and experiences you've had until this point. Now you've picked up another one, a curious one, see where it takes you, and listen to what you find there.

You've got the most incredible voice.

SO...WHAT SORCERY IS THIS?

WRITING PROMPTS AS A SIDE DOOR TO SELF-KNOWLEDGE.

Story Seeds is a collection of writing prompts designed to reveal your subconscious needs through the characters you create. Each prompt is a door of sorts. Your character walks through it, and in watching what they do, you learn a thing or two or three about yourself.

Side effects may include curing writer's block and creating whole new stories and characters that travel far beyond this realm.

It's not a replacement for therapy, but it can complement it, feel free to share it with your therapist...they'll probably find it fun and maybe it'll help them start that novel they've got inside them.

We've all got a novel inside us. Many novels. Every one of which is worth writing...especially the Harlequin ones. ;)

There's no need for perfect prose here either, you can polish it if that's your jam, but feel free to be as messy as you like, messy, and honest, and raw, and real.

Those are the essential base ingredients to cast any spell in this book.

And three eyes of newt.

A NOTE FOR WRITERS

THIS WORKS TWO WAYS...FOR THE HUMAN AND FOR YOUR FICTIONAL CHARACTER.

There are two ways to use this Grimoire, both are magical in their own right, and both can be used in tandem.

For the human holding the pen:

Your characters reveal YOUR needs. The barbarian who goes berserk? That's you longing to be wild and free. The rogue who trusts no one? That's your fear of betrayal, wearing a leather jacket and wielding a kukri.

For the writer crafting a story:

These same prompts can flesh out your characters' inner worlds. What does YOUR protagonist need? Run them through a seed and find out. Get some ideas from the needs that didn't come to the forefront. Open to a random page and point and see what comes of it. ;)

(And no, being a human and being a writer don't always go together. Some days we're just gremlins in mismatched socks who type.)

WHO DOES SHE THINK SHE IS?

MEET YOUR GUIDE.

Hi, I'm Stephen King, you may remember me from such novels as "The Shining" and "From a Buick 8." I wrote this Grimoire because— oh, no wait.. I'm not Stephen King, I'm Lily Rose. Silly me, I'm always confusing the two of us. I should probably explain. Many years ago I offered a snippet of writerly wisdom in the writing prompt group I helped run and one of the members responded with, "What do YOU know, are YOU Stephen King?" The subject we were discussing has long since left me, but those words have remained...haunted me, if you will. I laugh about them to this day. I'm laughing now as I write this.

As though Stephen King were the only person in the world capable of speaking on the subject, speaking "On Writing" if you'll forgive me. Mr. King would laugh along with me, I'd wager. Story is in our DNA as humans. Each of us is wise in our way simply for the life we've lived. Yes. Even THAT idiot you're thinking of right now. ;)

We don't need to create million dollar best sellers, hold a degree in creative writing, or have decades of roleplaying and character development under us to recognize good storytelling features.

It's our birthright.

However, if you're curious as to why I am OBSESSED with this stuff to the point of making this Grimoire, I'll tell you that I do have decades of experience running and playing in weekly table top roleplaying games, creating in-depth characters on paper and on the fly in the old school oral tradition of storytelling. Eddie Munson style.

And astrology transfixed me many moons ago, giving me the guidance I needed to navigate some very choppy waters. I've practiced it professionally for over a decade, including three beautiful years alongside two therapists with my own fancy office and everything. Astrology shows us our personal character sheet, the blueprint for our lives, and is a profoundly healing path to walk for those it resonates with.

I've also got a B.A. in English, so I learned what kills the joy of writing first hand...but also discovered the joy of "Things Fall Apart" by Chinua Achebe and analyzed every pixel of "The Breakfast Club" falling in love with the entire band of misfits.

I've penned and published psychological horror with King as my inspiration in countless books and magazines, across articles and essays, written comedy scripts in the style of Carol Burnett and scribed daily and monthly horoscopes through the eye of a raven. I've edited for Bram Stoker Award winners and my neighbor down the street who just wanted an eye on what he wrote. I've felt the soul of these writers through every story, every poem, every article. I've seen their hidden struggles and desires bleed through their characters and watched the profound healing that story can bring to writer and reader alike time and time and time again.

So, am I Stephen King? No. We've lived very different lives. But we've tapped into the same vein of wisdom.

And if you've read this far. So have you.

Now, if you trust me enough to guide you through this neat little Grimoire I pieced together, let's go hear what your soul has to say.

YEAH BUT, WHY DO I NEED THIS?

FOR WHEN YOU FINALLY ASK "WHAT DO I NEED?" AND HAVE NO IDEA.

People-pleasing. Putting others selflessly before you. Martyr in the First Degree. Perhaps it was for altruistic reasons, you cared for the person/people and so you sacrificed, or maybe survival dictated it or trauma molded it. Whatever the reason, you broke through with the enormous revelation that, at the end of the day, you need to put the focus on yourself and stop living your life for the external world.

"Great!" you say, "So I just need to ask for what I need." Sounds simple...but if you've spent a lifetime quieting your needs or maybe never being allowed to express them in the first place...you may stand there with your finger frozen triumphantly in the air and a lost expression in your eyes. "What...what do I need?"

You, in this moment of victory coupled with uncertainty, are why I wrote this Grimoire. To guide you in exploring this very worthy path you are stepping down. Wobbly steps are still steps. Crawling is still movement forward. And rest, well, rest is the ultimate act of rebellion..now isn't it? Kudos to you, this book isn't just a step, it's a hop and a skip and hopefully a little Irish Jig at the end.

Even seeing the path, when asked directly, "What are your needs?" you may balk, grow defensive, or revert to old familiar "shoulds." What society, tradition, family, or obligation say is what you "should" need. What you have a right to ask for or expect. And maybe there is some truth there, but maybe you need to explore this for yourself. Maybe you can come to see that what is needy or broken or too much to one person, fits you like a mad scientist's glove.

But getting past a lifetime of conditioning is a tricky gauntlet to run, which is where the Grimoire's magic comes in. When you ask, "What does my character do in a given situation, what do THEY need?" something altogether different happens. The question becomes safe, your defenses relax, and your subconscious, ever so patiently waiting for a chance to speak, lovingly guides you to the answer.

These prompts are a secret side entrance to self-knowledge. A way of accessing truths that direct questioning may not reach, at least not as quickly.

So what might your stories reveal? Let me show you.

THE NINE CORE NEEDS

THE MAP TO THE TREASURE WE'RE SEARCHING FOR.

I traveled the Nine Realms, gathering these needs, sometimes within a basket, sometimes as burrs stuck to my jacket and once...I lost a boot to the swamp to retrieve one of them. They're backed up through research, and people with letters behind their names, giants in many fields which I discuss at the end of this enchanted book. But through their wisdom and my raven's eye I've collected nine core needs that appear time and time again in our stories and our characters:

Safety & Security

The need to feel protected, grounded, & stable

Autonomy & Freedom

The need for sovereignty, choice, & independence

Connection & Belonging

The need to be seen, known, & welcomed

Understanding & Clarity

The need for things to make sense

Rest & Peace

The need to stop, release, & find stillness

Recognition & Significance

The need to matter, & be noticed

Expression & Creativity

The need to create, speak, & be heard

Purpose & Contribution

The need to serve something greater

Growth & Transformation

The need to evolve, become, & expand

Your stories will showcase these needs, sometimes one at a time, sometimes several woven in and out of each tale and character choice. The patterns that emerge across multiple prompts show what's most alive in you right now and those needs can and will shift over time.

These prompts are evergreen. Your needs are ever evolving.

HOW DO I CAST THIS SPELL?

THE SIMPLE RITUAL: READ, WRITE, REFLECT.

Read the prompt. Set a timer for 10 minutes. Write whatever comes and try not to overthink it. When the timer ends, stop (or keep going if you're in flow). Read what you wrote. Then use the interpretation guide that follows each prompt to discover what your story may be telling you about what your needs are.

That's it. No electrodes. No Ph.D required. Just you, a writing configuration, and ten minutes of free writing whatever you gosh darn please. There is no right or wrong to any of it. And no one is judging.

Except the newt.

Perhaps we should add "tongue of newt" to the ingredient list in the future then?

DO I NEED TO DO ALL 6?

NOPE.

Heavens no. If a single prompt illuminates your needs right now then by all means go forth and cultivate, explore, and integrate that need. Live your best life and maybe share this Grimoire with someone else who could benefit from it.

Or you may find value in doing a few prompts, each one diving into different parts of your psyche, revealing more about your needs or highlighting others. Or maybe this is helping you get past your writer's block, or explore a character in more detail, and that's cool too. Not everything needs to be a Jungian playground.

That said, needs do change and shift so you may find it helpful to return to these prompts when you know something is amiss in your life and need some help figuring out what that might be. Let the Grimoire be a living record of your evolution.

AND ONE MORE THING...

SOME TRAIL MIX FOR THE ROAD.

Multiple needs can be shown. Your story may very well highlight several needs at once. That's normal, we're complex creatures who wear clothes and play Candy Crush. All the needs are important but notice if one is louder than the others and perhaps address that one first.

Needs are also complex and may be at odds with one another. The need for freedom AND connection, craving rest AND growth. The struggle is real. Naming it is the first step toward getting them to play nice together.

Not every bullet point has to match. When you read the interpretation guide for each need, you don't have to check every box. If even one line makes you pause, that's signal enough.

Did nothing resonate? That's data too. You may not have any pressing needs right now and things are going great. If so, celebrate that and I hope the writing prompt sparked a good idea at the very least. Or perhaps you're resisting knowing your needs right now, which could warrant further reflection through other healing modalities, should you so choose to go down another rabbit hole.

Now. Find a comfortable spot. This is a ten minute prompt but the interpretation can take longer, up to an hour or more. This time is just for you. Let yourself write without judging (nuts to the newt!). And give yourself time and space afterwards to reflect.

Not because you NEED to...but because you're worth it.

Let's plant some seeds and see what grows.

STORY SEED #1: THE MOVED THING

The Prompt:
Your character comes home to find one thing moved from where they left it. What is it? What do they do?

Grab your pen, your laptop, and your writing appendage of choice. Set your timer. Ten minutes. Go.

Welcome back. Let's discover what your story has to say.

HARVEST GUIDE

What Sprouted?

The Object: What was moved? Was it practical (keys, wallet, tools) or sentimental (photo, letter, gift)? Was it valuable, secret, or ordinary? Did it belong to your character, or to someone else?

The Response: What did your character do FIRST? Were they frightened, angry, curious, or something else? Did they feel invaded, or did part of them hope someone had been there?

The Suspicion: Who (if anyone) did they think moved it? Did they want to find that person, or avoid them?

The Resolution: Did they investigate or try to ignore it? Did they tell anyone or keep it to themselves? Did the story end with answers or with lingering uncertainty?

The Nine Needs

Read through each need below. Notice what resonates. Notice what you resist.

Once your needs are identified, skip to the Needs Compendium for a deeper dive.

1. SAFETY & SECURITY

Your story might reveal this need if:

- Your character immediately checked the doors, windows, or exits
- Your character searched for weapons or ways to defend themselves
- Your character felt their space had been violated or contaminated
- Your character couldn't relax until they'd checked everywhere
- The moved object was something related to protection (keys, locks, phone)
- Fear was the dominant emotion
- Your character was hypervigilant to every sound afterward

Getting to the root:

Notice what comes up when you consider your edges...the places where you end and others begin. Are there spaces that feel fully yours right now? Spaces that don't?

Let yourself imagine, just for a moment, what "secure" might feel like in your body. What's there? What would help you feel more secure right now?

Maybe there was a time you felt truly held. If something surfaces, stay with it a breath. What made it so?

Real-world cultivation:

What's one small thing you could do this week to feel more grounded? This might be physical (fix that lock, create a cozy corner) or emotional (set a boundary, limit contact with someone who destabilizes you).

Give it a try and even if it sits on the tip of your tongue and you almost do it, that is progress, so give yourself grace and come at it again next time.

2. AUTONOMY & FREEDOM

Your story might reveal this need if:

- Your character felt ANGRY that someone touched their things
- The violation was about someone being in their space without permission
- Your character's first thought was "who would dare?"
- The moved object was something personal, something that was THEIRS
- Your character resented having to deal with this, having their routine disrupted
- Boundaries were a central theme
- Your character wanted to reclaim control immediately
- Your character longed to escape, leave, start somewhere untouched

Getting to the root: Let yourself wonder... where does your life feel fully yours right now? Where does it feel like you're living in response to someone else's choices?

Notice if anything tightens when you ask: whose permission am I waiting for? Is it permission I actually need, or permission I've been trained to seek?

What would it feel like to simply... decide? Without consulting, or defending, or explaining.

Real-world cultivation: Where might you reclaim even a small corner of sovereignty this week? This could be saying no to something, making a choice without polling others, or simply doing one thing YOUR way without apology. Even noticing where you hold back is progress. Name it. Knowledge is power and that is a beautiful beginning.

3. CONNECTION & BELONGING

Your story might reveal this need if:

- Your character's first thought was WHO had been there, not what they wanted
- Your character felt a flash of hope... maybe it was someone they missed
- The moved object connected to a relationship (a gift, a photo, something shared)
- Loneliness or isolation colored the scene
- Part of them wished someone HAD been there
- Your character immediately wanted to tell someone about it
- The story referenced someone from the past with longing
- Your character called out, or checked for signs of a specific person

Getting to the root: Notice who came to mind as you wrote. Was there someone you hoped had been in that space? Someone you wished would show up unannounced, just to see you?

Let yourself wonder... where do you feel most welcomed right now? Where do you feel like you're on the outside, looking in?

What would it mean to be truly seen by someone, not some curated version of you, but the real one? What if that someone... was you?

Real-world cultivation: Is there anyone who makes you feel seen that you could move toward this week? A text, a call, a coffee. Or maybe it's softer than that, just letting yourself miss someone without judging the missing. Connection doesn't always start with action. Sometimes it starts with admitting the longing.

And how might you cultivate a sense of belonging within yourself? A party of one... yes, but the most important party you'll ever attend.

4. UNDERSTANDING & CLARITY

Your story might reveal this need if:

- Your character immediately tried to figure out HOW and WHY
- Your character searched for clues, evidence, explanations
- Not knowing was intolerable and they HAD to understand
- The mystery mattered more than the threat
- Your character replayed events, trying to make it make sense
- Resolution (or lack of it) was the emotional center of the story
- Your character rationalized, theorized, or created explanations
- Your character doubted their own memory or perception

Getting to the root: What in your life right now doesn't quite make sense? Let yourself sit with that for a moment... the unsolved thing, the question that gnaws at you or hums in the background.

Notice how your body responds to not-knowing. Is there tightness? Restlessness? Increased heart rate? What would it feel like to have that one answer fall into your lap?

And gently... is there something you're afraid to understand? A rug you'd rather not look under, because seeing what's there might change everything?

Real-world cultivation: Is there one thing you've been avoiding looking at directly? Perhaps a question you might ask, a conversation you could initiate, a truth you may finally let yourself see? You don't have to resolve it this week. But maybe you could turn toward it, just slightly. A hair is still a measurement of movement.

5. REST & PEACE

Your story might reveal this need if:

- Your character was EXHAUSTED by the disruption
- The moved object represented order, routine, predictability
- Your character's primary feeling was "I don't have the energy for this"
- Your character wanted to restore normalcy more than find answers
- The story had a quality of weariness, of being too tired for one more thing
- Your character wished they could ignore it and just rest
- Peace was more important than justice or answers
- There was longing for simpler times

Getting to the root: Notice what you're carrying right now. Not only the to-do list, but the weight underneath it, the ongoing kettlebell of effort that never stops swinging.

When did you last truly rest? Not collapse-from-exhaustion rest, but the kind where you actually let go. If nothing comes to mind, that's information too.

What would you need to set down... even temporarily...just a few moments...I swear... to feel some peace?

Real-world cultivation: What's one thing you could take off your plate this week, or let be "good enough" instead of perfect? Yes, really. Breathe. Not everything has to be perfect. I say this as a Virgo so know it comes from a genuine place.

Rest isn't always sleep. Sometimes it's just... stopping. Letting the dishes sit. Saying "not today." Give yourself one pocket of peace, even five minutes. You've earned it simply by existing, not by finishing the list. Humans aren't here to be productive, otherwise we'd be human producings. Which sounds disturbing doesn't it?

Because it is.

6. RECOGNITION & SIGNIFICANCE

Your story might reveal this need if:

- The moved object represented their identity or achievements
- Your character felt unseen, as though even their own space didn't acknowledge them
- The intrusion felt like being erased or dismissed
- Your character wondered if they even mattered to whoever did this
- There was a quality of "does anyone see me? Does anyone notice?"
- Your character wanted acknowledgment, even from the intruder
- The violation felt less about safety and more about being disregarded
- Your character struggled to see themselves clearly in the scene

Getting to the root: Let yourself wonder... where in your life do you feel fully seen right now? Where do you feel invisible, passed over, or taken for granted?

Whose recognition have you been waiting for? Sit with that name, that face, for a moment. Why theirs?

And gently — what would it feel like to truly know, in your bones, that you matter? Not because of what you do, but because you exist. What if that recognition came from within you first and everyone else after?

Real-world cultivation: Yeah, let's roll with that a moment longer. What if you didn't wait for someone else to see you this week? Write down three things you did that mattered, even and most especially, small things. Say them out loud and write them down and look at them. Use lipstick on the mirror if you like. Give yourself the acknowledgment you've been waiting for. It counts when it comes from you. In fact, it counts the utmost. Shiny and sparkly and full of fire.

7. EXPRESSION & CREATIVITY

Your story might reveal this need if:

- The moved object was something creative, art, writing, an instrument, sculpture, etc...
- Your character processed the disruption by creating, writing, or talking through it
- There was a need to TELL someone or narrate the experience
- Your character felt silenced or stifled by the mystery
- The story itself became elaborate, vivid, richly detailed and maybe — *hopefully* — you couldn't stop writing
- Your character felt like they were choking on words they couldn't say
- The first impulse was to document, record, or express what happened, perhaps spelled out in bright candy on the roof.

Getting to the root: Notice what's been trying to come through you lately. A story, a conversation, a feeling that keeps pressing at your edges.

Where do you feel most free to express yourself right now? Where do you feel muted, edited, or held back?

Is there something you've been rehearsing in your head that's never made it out of your mouth? Let it surface, even for a moment. Even in candy form. Especially then.

Real-world cultivation: What's one small creative act you could take this week, with no purpose other than letting something out? Write the messy thing. Continue this prompt and see where it takes you/your character. Sing in the car, in the shower, in the grocery store. Doodle in the margins or make all the "O's" into smileys or Santas or... Say the thing you've been thinking, to whoever needs to hear it, and/or to yourself.

Expression doesn't need to be polished, it's already shiny when it comes out. It simply needs to move from inside to outside.

Oh yes, and have fun with it, whatever it is. And send me a copy or a pic if you're so inclined. It would make my day…just don't let that be the REASON for you creating… do it for you.

8. PURPOSE & CONTRIBUTION

Your story might reveal this need if:

- Your character immediately thought about protecting someone else
- The moved object represented their role, their usefulness, their function
- Your character's first response was to fix, solve, or manage for others
- There was concern about others being affected (family, roommates, neighbors)
- Your character wanted to warn, protect, or serve
- The story touched on legacy, what they're FOR, what they leave behind
- Your character felt useless or adrift in the face of the disruption
- They only felt okay once they had something to DO about it

Getting to the root: Let yourself ask, softly... what am I here for? Not what you've been told, not what's expected, what YOU feel, underneath all the noise.

Who benefits from your existence? (And are you on that list? I'll wait while you add yourself. Okay, good.)

Notice if there's a role you've been playing that no longer fits or suits you. Or a calling you've been ignoring because it seems impractical, or too big, or too small.

Real-world cultivation: What's one way you could contribute this week that would feel genuinely meaningful, not obligatory, but alive? It doesn't have to be grand. Sometimes purpose is just showing up for someone, making something, planting something, sending a smiley emote randomly. Let it be small. Small still counts.

9. GROWTH & TRANSFORMATION

Your story might reveal this need if:

- Your character saw the disruption as a sign, a catalyst, or a call to change
- The moved object represented an old version of themselves
- Your character was ready to leave something behind
- The story touched on becoming, evolving, shedding old skin
- There was restlessness, a sense of being ready for something new
- The disruption felt like an invitation, not just a violation
- Your character longed to be transformed by the experience
- What happened felt like the universe nudging them awake

Getting to the root: Notice what's stirring in you. Is there a version of yourself trying to emerge, one you haven't fully let in yet?

What have you outgrown that you're still carrying? A belief, a role, a relationship, or any story about who you are?

If you trusted that growth was safe, that you would land on your feet no matter what... what would you do next?

Real-world cultivation: What's one small step you could take toward the person you're becoming? Not a leap. A step. Read that book? Send that message? Say those words? Let go of that one thing. You don't have to have it all figured out. Growth isn't a destination, think of it like the next honest move you can make. The one that feels right in your soul. Can you trust yourself to have your back? Can you trust that your future self will be equipped to deal with and maybe even THRIVE in whatever comes after?

. . .

What Your Story Revealed

Take a moment to reflect.

The need(s) that resonated most:

What surprised me about what I wrote:

What my character wanted that I might want too:

One small thing I could do to honor this need:

grief, confusion, or existential dread? Did they hold it tenderly or at arm's length? Did finding it feel like a gift or an ambush?

The Choice: What did they do with it? Keep it, chuck it out the window, return it from whence it came, or decide to give it away? Did they tell anyone about what they found?

The Memory: What came flooding back? A person, a time, a version of themselves they'd forgotten existed?

THE NINE NEEDS

Read through each need below. Notice what resonates. Notice what you resist. Once your needs are identified, skip to the Needs Compendium for a deeper dive.

1. SAFETY & SECURITY

Your story might reveal this need if:

- The forgotten object felt dangerous to rediscover
- Your character wanted to hide it again, quickly, before anyone saw
- Finding it triggered anxiety, vigilance, or a need to protect themselves
- The object connected to a time when they weren't safe
- Your character felt exposed, like a secret had been unearthed
- There was an urge to destroy it so it could never see the light of day again
- The closet itself felt like a boundary that had been breached, or a container that was no longer doing its job

Getting to the root: What have you tucked away for safekeeping that might not be keeping you safe anymore? Sometimes we hide things to protect ourselves, and sometimes those hidden things start to fester.

Notice if there's something you've buried that still has weight. Not to dig it up necessarily, but just to acknowledge it's there. What would it mean to feel safe enough to look at it?

Real-world cultivation: Is there something you've been avoiding because looking at it feels threatening? You don't have to excavate your whole past this week. But maybe you could open one small drawer, literal or metaphorical, and just... notice what's there. You can close it again. You're in charge of what gets examined and when. But most things look a lot less scary when we look at them in the light, and from many different angles.

2. AUTONOMY & FREEDOM

Your story might reveal this need if:

- The object represented a time when your character had fewer choices
- Finding it sparked resentment about who they used to be, or who others expected them to be
- Your character wanted to throw it away as an act of liberation
- The object belonged to a role they no longer want to play
- There was anger at past-self for keeping it, or at someone else for giving it to them
- The discovery felt like being pulled backward into a life they've outgrown
- Your character felt trapped by the memories attached to it

Getting to the root: Let yourself wonder... is there an old version of you that's still taking up space in your life? Old expectations, old roles, old "shoulds" that you've shoved in a closet but never actually released?

What would it feel like to finally let something go? Not because you have to, but because you're ready. Because it's yours to release, and you trust your own wings to carry you.

Real-world cultivation: Maybe this week you could let go of one thing. A physical object that ties you to who you were instead of who you're becoming. An old commitment that no longer fits. A belief about yourself that you've outgrown. Donate it, delete it, drop it like a hot potato. Feel the space that opens up. Breathe into it.

. . .

3. CONNECTION & BELONGING

Your story might reveal this need if:

- The object connected to someone they've lost or drifted from
- Finding it triggered longing for a person, a group, or a time of belonging
- Your character wanted to reach out to someone because of what they found
- The object was a gift, a letter, a photo, or something shared
- There was grief for a connection that no longer exists
- Your character wondered if the other person still had their matching piece, memory, or half of the story
- Loneliness colored the discovery

Getting to the root: Who came to mind when you wrote this? Whose hands touched this object before your character buried it? Is there someone you've let slip away that part of you still reaches for?

And gently... have you buried parts of yourself alongside those old connections? Versions of you that only existed in relationship with certain people?

What would it mean to belong to yourself, first and foremost, even as you miss them?

Real-world cultivation: Is there someone you could reach out to this week? Not necessarily the person from the object, but someone you've let drift. A text that says "I was thinking about you." Or maybe the cultivation is softer: letting yourself grieve a connection that's truly gone, without rushing past the ache. Sometimes honoring what was IS the connection.

Is there a group you might join? Online, or in your hometown? And how might you reconnect with yourself? Some thoughtful time on a walk, at the beach, or the spa? Five minutes of deep breathing as you realize you are reconnecting with yourself by virtue of doing this exercise. That's something special right there.

. . .

4. UNDERSTANDING & CLARITY

Your story might reveal this need if:

- Your character couldn't remember how they got the object, or why they kept it
- The discovery raised more questions than answers
- Your character became obsessed with reconstructing the story behind the object
- There was a sense of "who WAS I when this mattered to me?"
- The object challenged their current narrative about their past
- Your character needed to understand before they could decide what to do
- Confusion, or disorientation was a dominant feeling

Getting to the root: Is there a chapter of your own past that doesn't quite make sense to you? A time you've never fully understood, or a decision you made that you still can't explain?

Notice how it feels to have gaps in your own story. Are there parts of your history you've forgotten on purpose? Parts that got foggy because looking clearly was too painful? Or perhaps you transmuted that pain already into something else and that's where the gap comes from. It happens to me from time to time. There's just no RAM left for that file since it got converted to something else.

Real-world cultivation: You don't have to understand everything about your past. But if there's something nagging at you, maybe this week you could take one small step toward clarity. Look at old photos. Write down what you remember. Ask someone who was there. Or simply sit with the not-knowing, and notice that you survive it. Maybe it only holds the power over you that you give it...

5. REST & PEACE

Your story might reveal this need if:

- Your character was exhausted by the emotional weight of the discovery
- The primary wish was to put it back and forget they ever saw it
- Cleaning the closet was already overwhelming before this happened
- Your character thought "I don't have the bandwidth for this right now"
- There was longing for a simpler time, before things got complicated
- Peace mattered more than resolution
- The object represented unfinished business they don't have energy to finish

Getting to the root: Notice if the forgotten thing in your story is also a heavy thing. Are there old matters you haven't dealt with simply because you're too tired? Not avoiding, exactly, just perpetually postponing because everything else takes precedence?

What would it mean to give yourself permission to leave some things buried? Not forever, but for now. Because rest is allowed. Because not everything has to be processed on a schedule.

Real-world cultivation: What if this week, instead of excavating your emotional closets, you just... rested? Let the forgotten things stay forgotten a little longer. Closed a door instead of opening one. Chose peace over productivity. Lay on the floor with your feet up the wall and did absolutely nothing about anything. Revolutionary, I know.

6. RECOGNITION & SIGNIFICANCE

Your story might reveal this need if:

- The object represented an achievement, an award, or proof of something they accomplished
- Your character had forgotten they were once someone who mattered in a particular way
- Finding it felt like finding proof of their own existence, their own value

- There was grief that no one else remembers, or knows, or saw
- The object connected to a version of themselves they're proud of
- Your character wondered "why did I bury this? Why did I let myself forget I was this person?"
- The discovery was bittersweet because it highlighted how unseen they feel now

Getting to the root: What have you let yourself forget about your own significance (You splendid human creature you...)? What evidence of your own value have you shoved in a closet, minimized, or otherwise stopped talking about?

Why do we do that? Why do we hide our own proof of worth?

Let yourself wonder... what would it mean to display that forgotten thing proudly? To let it be seen?

Real-world cultivation: Dig something out this week. A photo from a profound moment. An old award or certificate. A piece of writing or art you made. Something that proves you've done things that mattered. Put it somewhere you can see it. Let it remind you. You don't have to be modest about who you've been. That person was real, and so is the one you're becoming. And if there is nothing, give yourself a grand, silly, and wondrous title like Eldritch Horror of the Month.

7. EXPRESSION & CREATIVITY

Your story might reveal this need if:

- The object was something creative: old writing, art, music, a journal, a half-finished project
- Finding it sparked a longing to create again
- Your character felt grief for the creative self they used to be
- There was shame about abandoning the whatsit.
- The object proved they once had time, energy, or permission for creativity
- Your character wanted to pick it back up, or put it down the disposal so they wouldn't have to think about what they gave up

- The forgotten thing was a voice they stopped using

Getting to the root: What creative part of yourself have you buried? What expressive self got shoved in a closet when life got busy, or hard, or when someone told you it wasn't practical?

Is that self still in there, waiting? Do they have something to say? I think I hear them now... something like a high-speed train.

Real-world cultivation: Maybe this week you could dust off one abandoned creative thing. Not to finish it or make it perfect, but just to say hello. To let that part of you know you remember them. Play the instrument badly. Read the old writing without cringing. Everything you make has its own beauty, even if it needs a few passes of your editor's eye. Make something new and terrible and alive. Have it breathe the fire that's within you!

8. PURPOSE & CONTRIBUTION

Your story might reveal this need if:

- The object represented a path not taken, or an abandoned calling
- Finding it raised questions about what your character is supposed to be doing with their life
- The object connected to a time when they felt useful, purposeful, or needed
- There was grief for a mission they walked away from
- Your character wondered if they could still pick up that thread, or if it's too late
- The discovery felt like a rebuke from their past self
- The object was something meant to be given to someone else, or passed down, or finished

Getting to the root: What purpose have you set aside? What calling got buried under the demands of survival mode and the hue of emergency lighting?

Is it still calling? Softly, from the back of the closet? What would it mean to answer, even partially, even imperfectly?

Real-world cultivation: Take one small action this week toward something that feels purposeful. Not the whole enchilada. Just one bite in a direction that matters to you. Write one paragraph. Make one call. Plant one seed. Purpose doesn't require grand gestures. It just needs to be fed... or eaten, a little at a time. For more inspiration see "The Whale" by Shel Silverstein.

9. GROWTH & TRANSFORMATION

Your story might reveal this need if:

- The object represented who your character used to be, and how far they've come
- Finding it triggered awareness of their own evolution
- Your character barely recognized the person who owned that thing
- There was pride in outgrowing it, or grief for innocence lost
- The discovery felt like meeting a past self and realizing they've transformed
- Your character saw the object as proof they've changed
- The forgotten thing belongs to a chapter that's truly closed, or maybe ready to close

Getting to the root: Let yourself feel the distance between who you were and who you are now. Big or small. That's growth. That's survival. That's thousands of choices, stacked up, leading you here.

What have you outgrown that you're still carrying? Like arm floaties long after you've learned the butterfly stroke. What could you finally release, knowing that letting go doesn't erase where you've been?

Real-world cultivation: Find something this week that represents who you used to be. Hold it. Thank it for getting you to this point. Then decide: does this come with you into the next chapter? Or does it stay behind? Either answer is right. The growth is in the asking.

WHAT YOUR STORY REVEALED

Take a moment to reflect.

The need(s) that resonated most:

What surprised me about what I wrote:

What my character wanted that I might want too:

One small thing I could do to honor this need:

STORY SEED #3: THE SILENT DINNER

The Prompt:
Your character sits across from someone at a holiday dinner. Neither has spoken to the other in years. What happens in the silence?

Grab your pen, your laptop, and your writing appendage of choice. Set your timer. Ten minutes. Go.

Welcome back. How was the food? Let's discover what your story has to say.

HARVEST GUIDE

What Sprouted?

The Other Person: Who was across the table? Family, former friend, ex-partner, or someone else? What history sits between them? What caused the silence in the first place?

The Silence: What lived in that quiet? Anger, grief, longing, resent-

ment, shame, or something harder to name? Did the silence feel like a wall, a wound, or a strange kind of intimacy?

The Almost: Was there a moment where one of them almost spoke? What stopped them? What were the words caught in their throat?

The Outcome: Did the silence break, or hold? Did anything pass between them without words? Did your character leave the dinner with more weight on their chests or less? Figuratively or literally?

THE NINE NEEDS

Read through each need below. Notice what resonates. Notice what you resist. Once your needs are identified, skip to the Needs Compendium for a deeper dive.

1. SAFETY & SECURITY

Your story might reveal this need if:

- Your character felt unsafe in the other person's presence
- The silence was protective, a shield against potential harm
- Your character was hyperaware of the other person's movements, tone, or expressions
- There was a history of volatility, and the silence kept things from exploding
- Your character wanted to leave, to escape, to be anywhere else
- The holiday setting felt like a trap, forcing proximity that wasn't chosen
- Speaking felt too dangerous, so silence was the only safe option

Getting to the root: Are there people in your life whose presence puts your nervous system on alert? Relationships where silence feels safer than honesty?

Notice what your body does when you imagine sitting across from someone who has hurt you. Is there armor? Tension? A practiced blankness that protects? A grey rock?

What would safety actually require in that relationship? Is it possible there, or only in distance?

Real-world cultivation: You don't have to reconcile with everyone. You don't have to break every silence. Some silences are boundaries. Some distance is protection. If there's a relationship where you've been pressuring yourself to "fix things," ask yourself honestly: is repair possible AND safe? If not, your silence might be wisdom, not avoidance. Breath is life, and life is precious.

2. AUTONOMY & FREEDOM

Your story might reveal this need if:

- Your character resented being forced into this situation by family obligation or social expectation
- The silence was partly defiance, a refusal to perform reconciliation
- Your character felt trapped by the holiday, the table, or the expectations of others
- There was anger at having to share space with this person against their will
- Your character wanted to speak their truth but knew it would cause chaos, and they resented that bind
- The story touched on family roles and the exhaustion of playing them
- Your character longed to stand up and walk out

Getting to the root: Where in your life are you performing peace you don't feel? Where are you showing up out of obligation rather than choice? What family dynamics still have you playing a role that no longer fits?

What would it feel like to give yourself permission to skip the next dinner? Or to show up differently than expected?

Real-world cultivation: You get to decide which tables you sit at. That

might sound radical, but it's true. This week, notice where you're performing, tolerating, or showing up out of "should." Ask yourself: what would I choose, if I were truly free? You don't have to act on it yet. But discover the answer.

3. CONNECTION & BELONGING

Your story might reveal this need if:

- Your character desperately wanted to speak but didn't know how to bridge the gap
- The silence was painful precisely because this person once mattered so much
- Your character missed who this person used to be, or who they used to be together
- There was longing underneath the quiet, a wish for reconciliation or understanding
- The holiday setting highlighted what's been lost, the belonging that used to exist here
- Your character looked at others at the table who still had easy connection, and ached
- The silence felt like exile

Getting to the root: Who have you lost to silence? Not to death, but to distance, to words that were said or never said, to time that passed until reaching out felt impossible?

Is there grief under your estrangements? Not just anger or righteousness, but genuine mourning for connection that used to exist?

What would it mean to belong to yourself, even in the spaces where you've been cast out or walked away? Or to foster a sense of belonging in a wider sense. Such as belonging to humanity as a whole, to the Earth, to the Universe, or a god or goddess of your choice. To understand that people may walk with us for a time on our path, and then may take another, and that doesn't have to mean anyone has failed. We've simply taken different routes, to learn and see different things.

Real-world cultivation: If there's someone you miss, and if reaching

out is safe and wanted, maybe this week you could make one small move. Not to fix everything. Just to crack the door. "I've been thinking about you." "I miss how we used to be." Or if reconciliation isn't possible or healthy, let yourself grieve. That's honoring the connection too. Or take the wider view. Thank them for their time in your life and send them on their way with love. Wish them the best and look ahead on where your path is going now. Allow new possibilities to excite you.

4. UNDERSTANDING & CLARITY

Your story might reveal this need if:

- Your character wanted to understand what went wrong, or finally be understood themselves
- The silence was full of unanswered questions
- Your character replayed old arguments, old hurts, trying to make sense of them
- There was a desperate wish for the other person to finally SEE their perspective
- The story touched on misunderstanding, miscommunication, or things that were never explained
- Your character wanted to ask "why?" but knew they wouldn't get a real answer
- The silence felt like a refusal to engage, to explain, or to be knowable

Getting to the root: What relationship in your life still doesn't make sense to you? Where are you still waiting for an explanation, an apology, or an acknowledgment that may never come?

What would it mean to find your own understanding, even without their participation? To write your own meaning onto the silence?

Real-world cultivation: Some questions never get answered by the person who owes us answers. That's harsh, and real. But you can still find clarity. Write down what you know to be true about what happened. Write what you'll never know. Understand that they very well may have been projecting wounds onto you that you cannot see. It probably wasn't

personal. And they may not be capable of giving you closure. Can you radically accept what is, here and now? And let go and grieve what no longer will be? Forgive them, understand they did the best they could with the life they've lived up until this point, and let go of the need to know. Let them keep their version so you can fly free.

5. REST & PEACE

Your story might reveal this need if:

- Your character was exhausted by the tension, performing calm while internally churning
- The silence was preferable to conflict because conflict takes energy they don't have
- Your character just wanted to get through the dinner and go home
- There was longing for simpler times, holidays that weren't minefields
- Peace mattered more than justice or resolution
- Your character didn't want to fight, explain, or process. They just wanted it to be over
- The emotional labor of the estrangement has been grinding them down

Getting to the root: Are there relationships in your life that exhaust you to even think about? Dynamics where you spend more energy managing your own reactions than actually connecting?

What would peace look like for you? Not resolution necessarily. Just... peace. Is that possible in this relationship, or only far away from it?

Real-world cultivation: Give yourself permission to want peace more than reconciliation. Those aren't the same thing. Sometimes the most loving thing you can do for yourself is stop trying to fix something that just keeps cutting your hands. Rest from the effort. The dinner will happen without your emotional labor holding it together. Let go of control of and responsibility for it. Trust that things will unfold as they will.

. . .

6. RECOGNITION & SIGNIFICANCE

Your story might reveal this need if:

- Your character wanted to be seen, acknowledged, or finally heard by this person
- The silence felt like erasure, like being treated as invisible or unimportant
- Your character wanted the other person to recognize the hurt they caused
- There was a sense of "do I even matter to them anymore?"
- Your character wondered if they'd been forgotten, replaced, or dismissed
- The story touched on being the one who reaches out, who tries, while the other person doesn't bother
- Recognition from this specific person felt necessary for closure

Getting to the root: Whose recognition are you still waiting for? Whose acknowledgment would finally let you exhale?

And what if it never comes? What if they never see it, never admit it, never give you what you deserve?

Can you recognize yourself in the absence of their witness? Can you see the value in the experience, even if no one else does?

Real-world cultivation: If they won't recognize you, recognize yourself. Know that what you've given, or done was worthy of recognition, but for whatever reason the other person wasn't able to give it. Some people have busted receivers, it makes it hard for them to see themselves as worthy of being given to and so they have blinders on to those who give and give and give.

Try asking directly for that recognition. It could be the person doesn't realize they haven't been showing it, or showing it in a way you can receive. A love language you speak. Don't assume malicious intent. Ask gently. And if it is still denied then ask yourself if this is a dynamic you want to continue. But your significance doesn't depend on their seeing it. You are worthy simply for existing. Be your own witness. Let the giving be beautiful and embrace what it says about the beauty within you.

7. EXPRESSION & CREATIVITY

Your story might reveal this need if:

- Your character had so much to say and no way to say it
- The silence felt like choking, like being muzzled
- Your character rehearsed speeches in their head, perfect words they couldn't deliver
- There was frustration at not being able to express the full truth
- The story explored the gap between what's felt and what's spoken
- Your character wanted to write a letter, scream, or finally let it all out
- The silence was unbearable because expression was impossible

Getting to the root: What have you never been able to say to someone who needed to hear it? What words are still lodged in your throat, years later?

Is there a way to express them, if not to that person, then somewhere? The words want out. They don't necessarily need the intended recipient. Many a grand novel has come of such expression.

Real-world cultivation: Write the letter you'll never send. Say the thing out loud to an empty chair. Let your journal hold what they refused to hear. The expression doesn't need to reach them to heal you. It just needs to move from inside to outside. Let it out. It's been in there long enough. And dance, or exercise, or do some yoga. Move the emotion and frustration through your body and don't let it trouble you a minute longer. You've got a world to create. Your own.

. . .

8. PURPOSE & CONTRIBUTION

Your story might reveal this need if:

- Your character felt responsible for fixing the rift, holding the family together, or being the bigger person
- The silence represented a failure, something they couldn't repair despite trying
- Your character wanted to contribute to healing but didn't know how
- There was guilt about the estrangement, even if they weren't solely responsible
- Your character took on the emotional labor of the whole table, empathic as they are
- The story touched on roles: the peacekeeper, the scapegoat, the fixer
- Your character's sense of purpose was wrapped up in this relationship working

Getting to the root: Have you made someone else's healing your responsibility? Have you assigned yourself a role in a relationship that isn't yours to carry?

What would it mean to let go of being the one who fixes it? To trust that your purpose isn't to perform miracles at dinner tables with badly hemmed tablecloths drooping on one side?

Real-world cultivation: Notice this week where you're over-functioning in relationships. Where you're trying to heal rifts that aren't yours to heal. Put down one burden that belongs to someone else. Let them carry it, or let it sit. Your purpose isn't to save every sinking ship. Some ships you're allowed to let sail without you. You weren't heading in that direction anyway.

9. GROWTH & TRANSFORMATION

Your story might reveal this need if:

- Your character realized they've outgrown this dynamic, this person, or this version of family
- The silence marked a clear before-and-after in their life
- Your character saw the other person and recognized how much they themselves have changed
- There was grief for who they used to be together, and acceptance that it's over
- The story touched on evolution, on becoming someone who no longer fits at this table
- Your character felt ready to release this, even if it hurts
- The dinner felt like a final chapter, an ending acknowledged

Getting to the root: What relationships have you outgrown? What tables no longer have a seat that fits you? Maybe the leg is wobbly, or worse, it's a kid's chair and you're an adult hunched over in it.

Is there grief in that? Can growth and grief make good bedfellows?

What would it mean to let this relationship exist in the past tense, to honor what was without needing it to become something else? To understand you are on different paths now and that doesn't have to mean anyone was wrong. You've just grown in different directions.

Real-world cultivation: Let yourself acknowledge one relationship where you may have learned everything you can from each other, at least right now. Can you accept that you are taking one path and they another? That maybe in the future you'll meet again further on down and have stories to share. It doesn't have to take away anything that once was, keep the good memories and wish them well on their journey. Then look ahead with bright eyes to the new possibilities ahead.

WHAT YOUR STORY REVEALED

Take a moment to reflect.

The need(s) that resonated most:

What surprised me about what I wrote:

What my character wanted that I might want too:

One small thing I could do to honor this need:

STORY SEED #4: WHAT YOU CARRY

The Prompt:

Your character is traveling somewhere important. The bag is packed with the basics, no worries there, but they're holding one thing in their hands, deciding whether it fits. What is it, and why does it matter enough to make room?

Grab your pen, your laptop, and your writing appendage of choice. Set your timer. Ten minutes. Go.

Welcome back. Let's discover what your story has to say.

HARVEST GUIDE

What Sprouted?

The Object: What did they choose? Was it practical, sentimental, protective, or symbolic? Did it represent a person, a memory, a hope, or a fear? Or was there nothing at all... and what does THAT mean?

The Sacrifice: What, if anything, did they leave behind to make room for this one thing? Was that choice easy or agonizing? What almost made the cut?

The Destination: Where were they going? Toward something or away from something? Was the journey chosen or forced?

The Weight: How did they carry it? Close to their body, hidden away, or openly displayed? What did carrying this thing cost them? What did it give them?

THE NINE NEEDS

Read through each need below. Notice what resonates. Notice what resists. Once your needs are identified, skip to the Needs Compendium for a deeper dive.

1. SAFETY & SECURITY

Your story might reveal this need if:

- The object was protective: a weapon, a lock, a phone, money, or documents
- Your character chose something that would help them survive
- The journey felt dangerous, and the object was armor against threat
- Your character prioritized practical safety over sentiment
- There was anxiety about the destination and what they might face
- The object was something that makes them feel less alone, less vulnerable
- Security was more important than comfort or meaning

Getting to the root: When you imagine stepping into the unknown, what do you reach for? What makes you feel protected, even if it's just a feeling?

Notice if your character's choice was about physical safety or emotional safety. What does that tell you about what you're protecting yourself from?

Real-world cultivation: What do you actually need to feel secure right now? Not someday, not in theory. Right now. Is there something you've been avoiding putting in place: an emergency fund, a boundary, a plan? What's one small step you can take in that direction? Even writing it out makes it a little more real than it was yesterday.

2. AUTONOMY & FREEDOM

Your story might reveal this need if:

- The object represented independence: keys, money, their own transportation
- Your character chose something that meant they could take care of themselves
- The journey was about escape, and the object ensured they couldn't be pulled back
- Your character refused to bring something that tied them to others
- There was defiance in the choice, a refusal to be dependent
- The object symbolized self-sufficiency
- Freedom mattered more than comfort or connection
- Your character brought nothing at all, not from depletion, but from radical self-trust: they ARE the resource

Getting to the root: What do you need to carry to feel free? Is it an actual thing, or is it an internal quality: courage, permission, self-trust?

Notice if your character was traveling toward freedom or away from captivity. What are you trying to get free from? What would freedom actually look like, and what would you need to carry to get there?

And if your character brought nothing? Perhaps trusting themselves to find what they need when they get where they are going. That's sovereignty. That is freedom. That is beautiful.

Real-world cultivation: What's weighing you down right now that isn't yours to carry? What could you set down this week that would make you feel lighter and more free? Sometimes the most important thing isn't what we carry. It's what we refuse to carry anymore.

And consider: what would it feel like to travel with nothing but your trust in yourself? Not reckless. Not underprepared. Just... knowing you're enough. That you can meet whatever comes your way in the moment. That you don't need to plan for everything because you can't plan for everything anyway. What if your hands were empty because they're ready to receive, not because they've been emptied? ;) Hehe. Flip the script. Always, Love.

3. CONNECTION & BELONGING

Your story might reveal this need if:

- The object connected them to someone: a photo, a letter, a ring, a gift
- Your character was bringing a person with them in symbolic form
- The object represented home, not as a place, but as a feeling
- There was longing in the choice: I can't go without this piece of us
- Your character was traveling toward reunion, and the object was proof of the bond
- The thing wasn't practical at all, just deeply meaningful
- Love outweighed logic

Getting to the root: Who do you carry with you, even when they're not there? Whose love travels in your back pocket, your open heart, or your muscle memory?

And here's the harder question: do you carry yourself with the same reverence? Are you one of the connections worth making room for? Consider putting yourself at the top of that list. Pack yourself. ;)

Real-world cultivation: Connection isn't just about others. This week, carry something that reminds you of your own worth. If you can't think of anything, make something. Write yourself a note. Take a photo of your own face, smiling. Find a necklace or bracelet you fancy and wear it purely for you. You are worth carrying too. The most worthy. <3

. . .

4. UNDERSTANDING & CLARITY

Your story might reveal this need if:

- The object was informational: a map, a journal, an address, documentation
- Your character needed to understand where they were going, and this thing helped orient them
- The object held answers, or at least clues
- There was a mystery at the destination, and your character couldn't arrive without preparation
- Your character couldn't travel without knowing something first
- The object wasn't a thing but a question they were carrying to find the answer
- Clarity mattered more than comfort

Getting to the root: What questions are you carrying into your future? What do you need to understand before you can move forward?

Notice if your character was waiting for clarity before they could leave. Are you doing the same thing? What if understanding comes after the journey, not before? Spooky.

Real-world cultivation: Sometimes we pack questions instead of answers. That's okay. This week, let yourself move forward without complete understanding. Trust that the journey itself might be the answer. Or that you'll find it along the way, somewhere you least expected, most likely.

5. REST & PEACE

Your story might reveal this need if:

- The object was comforting: something soft, familiar, calming
- Your character needed peace more than practicality
- The object was a small mercy for a difficult journey
- There was weariness in your character, and this thing helped them breathe

- Your character prioritized their sanity over efficiency
- The object wasn't useful, just soothing
- Peace mattered more than being prepared

Getting to the root: What do you carry for comfort? What small mercies travel with you into hard things?

Notice if your character packed something soft in the middle of something hard. Have you been packing so much for everyone else's journey that you forgot to bring something comforting for yourself?

Real-world cultivation: Pack something just for your peace this week. Not useful. Not practical. Just soothing. A playlist that makes you exhale. A photo that makes you smile. Permission to nap. You carry so much for everyone else. Now, it's your time.

6. RECOGNITION & SIGNIFICANCE

Your story might reveal this need if:

- The object was proof of who they are: a credential, an award, a letter of reference
- Your character feared being unknown at the destination and brought evidence of their worth
- The object represented identity, something that says "I matter"
- There was anxiety about being seen, and this thing was reassurance
- Your character was bringing their best self in tangible form
- The object wasn't for survival, it was for significance
- Being recognized mattered more than being comfortable

Getting to the root: What do you carry to prove your worth? To yourself, or to others?

Could you arrive somewhere new with nothing and still know you matter? Could you trust yourself to be significant without the props?

Real-world cultivation: You are not your credentials. You are not your proof. This week, practice arriving somewhere without your resume, your accomplishments, or your evidence. Just show up as you. See if you still matter. (Spoiler: you do. You matter because you exist, not because of the card you carry.)

7. EXPRESSION & CREATIVITY

Your story might reveal this need if:

- The object was creative: a journal, an instrument, a sketchbook, a camera, a set of paints
- Your character needed to process what they would experience, and this thing helps them do that
- There was fear of being silenced, and this thing was their voice
- Your character's identity is tied to making things
- The object wasn't practical, it was essential in a different way
- Expression mattered more than efficiency

Getting to the root: What creative tools do you carry? What helps you express yourself when words alone aren't enough?

Could you create without the tools? Could your voice be the instrument? Your body the canvas? Your presence the art?

Real-world cultivation: Creativity doesn't require equipment. It can happen anywhere at any time with any medium. Make some potatoes dance at a diner, paint a Picasso with ketchup and mustard on a napkin, rearrange some rocks into a heart on the beach. Sing or dance, strike a ridiculous pose. Who is going to stop you? Creativity is your birthright. Let it loose.

8. PURPOSE & CONTRIBUTION

Your story might reveal this need if:

- The object was meant for someone else at the destination
- Your character was bringing something to give, to contribute, or to offer
- The object represented their usefulness, their role, their reason for going

- There was a task to complete, and the thing was essential to it
- Your character was traveling to serve, and this thing was how
- The object wasn't for them at all
- Contribution mattered more than personal comfort

Getting to the root: What do you carry in service of others? What do you bring to give away?

Did your character pack anything just for themselves? Are you allowed to travel for your own sake, or does the journey only count if you're useful to someone at the other end?

Real-world cultivation: You are not a delivery service. This week, notice if you're carrying only things to give away. Pack one thing that's just for you, something that serves the purpose of bringing YOU joy. You are allowed to be the destination, not simply the messenger.

9. GROWTH & TRANSFORMATION

Your story might reveal this need if:

- The object represented who they're becoming, not who they've been
- Your character was packing for a future version of themselves
- The object was a seed, a symbol, something aspirational
- There was intention in the choice: this is who I'm growing into
- Your character deliberately left behind things from their old version
- The object wasn't about the journey, it was about the arrival
- Transformation mattered more than security

Getting to the root: What are you packing for your future self? What belongs to who you're becoming, not who you've been?

Notice if your character was traveling light because growth requires it. Sometimes we have to empty the bag. Bring nothing but ourselves and our trust in our becoming.

Real-world cultivation: Travel light into your transformation this week. Look at what you're carrying and ask: does this belong to the person I'm turning into? Or is it luggage from an old life? You don't have to throw everything away. But you might loosen your grip on a few things. Let the journey shape you. Let yourself arrive different than you left.

One More Thing...

If your character emptied the whole bag and brought only this one thing... that's significant. That's a soul speaking loudly about priorities. Everything practical, everything sensible, everything expected was set aside for this ONE thing. That's not impractical. That's clarity.

And if the thing they were holding wasn't an object at all, if it was hope, or fear, or a promise, or a prayer, or a version of themselves they're trying to become... then you're already doing the deeper work. You're already listening to what matters.

And if there was nothing? If your character stared at the bag with room to spare and found nothing they would bring?

Notice where that comes from.

Empty hands from sovereignty looks like: "I trust myself to find what I need. I AM the resource. I can't plan for everything, and I don't need to. I'll find a way if need be." That's freedom. That's arrival as a whole person, trusting yourself, hands open and ready to receive abundance from the world around you.

Empty hands from depletion looks like: "There's nothing left of me worth packing. Nothing I want. Nothing that's mine. I'm being dragged somewhere I didn't choose, and I've stopped having preferences because preferences require a self, and I've put mine in storage just to survive." That's erosion. That's a soul that's been stripped to the bone.

Same image, vastly different roots.

If it was sovereignty, kudos, honor it. You don't need the props. Huzzah!

If it was depletion... I see you. That emptiness is a starting point to fill, not a failure. It's a signal that you've lost touch with your desires. That's where the healing begins: noticing the absence. Naming what's been lost. Wondering what took those desires away in the first place. And how you can take it back and rekindle your fire...

WHAT YOUR STORY REVEALED

Take a moment to reflect.

The need(s) that resonated most:

What surprised me about what I wrote:

What my character wanted that I might want too:

One small thing I could do to honor this need:

STORY SEED #5: THE UNEARTHED

The Prompt:
The thing your character buried is uncovered. What is it?

Grab your pen, your laptop, and your writing appendage of choice. Set your timer. Ten minutes. Go.

Welcome back. Let's discover what your story has to say. How gruesome did you get?

HARVEST GUIDE

What Sprouted?

The Buried Thing: What was uncovered? Was it literal (an object, a body, a box) or metaphorical (a secret, a memory, a truth)? Was it buried by your character, or by someone else? Was it hidden to protect or hidden to forget?

The Uncovering: How was it found? Did your character dig it up themselves, or did someone else? Was it an accident, an intention, or an inevitability? Were they alone when it surfaced?

The Response: What did your character feel when they saw it again? Relief, terror, grief, shame, vindication, or something stranger? Did they want to bury it again, or finally deal with it?

The Reckoning: What happens now that it's exposed? Who else will know? What changes?

THE NINE NEEDS

Read through each need below. Notice what resonates. Notice what resists. Once your needs are identified, skip to the Needs Compendium for a deeper dive.

1. SAFETY & SECURITY

Your story might reveal this need if:

- The buried thing represented danger, and its resurfacing threatens your character
- Exposure means vulnerability, harm, or the loss of protection
- Your character buried it to feel safe, and now that safety is compromised
- There was panic, fear, or the urgent need to hide it again
- The uncovering felt like being found, caught, or exposed
- Your character's security depended on this staying buried
- Someone dangerous might now learn what was hidden

Getting to the root: What have you buried for your own protection? What truths, memories, or secrets stay hidden because exposing them feels unsafe?

Notice if the threat is still real, or if you're still hiding from a danger that has passed. Sometimes we protect ourselves from tigers that have long since left the jungle. Or we forget that we've grown and can take on the tiger in ways we couldn't before.

Real-world cultivation: If there's something buried that you're still hiding out of fear, ask yourself: is the danger still present, or am I protecting myself from a ghost? You don't have to unearth everything. But maybe one small thing could come to light this week, safely, with someone you trust. Let it breathe. Do you feel lighter?

2. AUTONOMY & FREEDOM

Your story might reveal this need if:

- The buried thing was something your character chose to put behind them, and its return feels like a violation
- Someone else uncovered it without permission, overriding your character's choice
- The resurfacing traps them, forces their hand, or removes their options
- Your character buried it as an act of agency, and now that agency is undone
- There's anger at losing control over what's known about them
- The buried thing represents a past they intentionally left, a door they closed
- Freedom feels threatened by this return

Getting to the root: What have you put behind you that you fear being dragged back into? What past choices, identities, or circumstances have you buried, not to hide, but to move on from?

What would it mean to stay free even if someone digs it up? Can your present self hold your past without being consumed by it?

Real-world cultivation: Your past doesn't own you, even if it surfaces. This week, practice holding something old with new eyes. Acknowledge that it happened, that you've changed. Look at it AND stay in the present. That's freedom.

3. CONNECTION & BELONGING

Your story might reveal this need if:

- The buried thing connected to a relationship: a letter, a gift, a shared secret, or something from someone lost
- Your character buried it because the connection was too painful to face
- The uncovering brings grief, longing, or the ghost of belonging
- Someone else finds out and now knows your character differently, for better or worse
- There's fear of being rejected, cast out, or seen as unworthy because of what was hidden
- The buried thing was a piece of intimacy your character couldn't carry anymore
- Connection is at stake depending on what happens next

Getting to the root: What have you hidden from the people who love you? What do you fear they'd think if they knew? Is it founded, or catastrophic thinking?

Have you buried parts of yourself to stay in belonging? What would it mean if they saw the whole you, including the buried parts?

And if you've buried something precious because it hurt too much to hold, are you ready to grieve it now?

Real-world cultivation: Consider sharing one hidden thing with someone safe this week. Not your deepest secret necessarily. Just one small truth you've tucked away. Are you still loved afterward? Or did the worst happen? Remember, you always belong to yourself and those who can't hold you may not be your tribe... and maybe that's okay.

4. UNDERSTANDING & CLARITY

Your story might reveal this need if:

- The buried thing was information, evidence, or proof of something long suspected
- Your character has been waiting for this to surface to confirm what they knew
- The uncovering brings clarity, answers questions, or exposes lies

- There was relief in finally KNOWING, even if the truth is hard
- Your character buried something because they couldn't understand it, and now it demands understanding
- The story touched on secrets that distorted reality, and now reality can be seen clearly
- Understanding is the gift of the unearthing, even if it hurts
- Your character went to unearth something and it wasn't there

Getting to the root: What truth have you buried because you weren't ready to understand it? What's waiting in your own ground to be seen clearly?

Is there something you already know but haven't let yourself fully know yet? Or maybe what you thought was there wasn't the same as you left it? Has time changed and softened things? What happens when you revisit them with fresh eyes? Preferably yours... in your sockets.

Real-world cultivation: Turn toward one buried truth this week. Not to excavate your whole history. Just to look at one thing you've avoided understanding. Let it be true. See what happens when you stop pretending you don't know what you know. Learn what you have unlearned.

5. REST & PEACE

Your story might reveal this need if:

- The buried thing was supposed to stay buried, and now your character has no peace
- Unearthing it means more work, more processing, more effort
- Your character buried it precisely so they could rest, and now rest is over
- There was exhaustion at the thought of dealing with this again
- Peace was purchased by burying, and the price is now due
- Your character just wants to bury it again and walk away
- The buried thing represents unfinished business that drains them

Getting to the root: What have you buried so you could have peace? Is that peace real, or did you postpone a reckoning?

Notice if there are things under the surface that are stealing your rest even while hidden. Sometimes the burying itself is exhausting.

Real-world cultivation: Sometimes the most restful thing is to finally deal with something. Not today necessarily. What's the cost of keeping that buried business buried? Your peace? Is it worth it?

6. RECOGNITION & SIGNIFICANCE

Your story might reveal this need if:

- The buried thing was something your character wanted to be known for, or never known for
- Exposure changes how others see them, for better or worse
- There was anxiety about legacy, reputation, or identity being disrupted
- Your character buried proof of who they really are, or who they used to be
- The uncovering forces others to recognize something they'd ignored or dismissed
- Your character has been waiting for this to be seen, or dreading it
- What surfaces demands acknowledgment

Getting to the root: What have you buried that's actually part of who you are? What truths about yourself have you hidden from recognition?

Are there parts of you waiting to be seen? Parts you've deemed too shameful, too much, or too strange to ever see the light of day?

Real-world cultivation: Let something buried be seen this week. A talent you've hidden. A truth you've minimized. A part of yourself you've kept underground. You don't have to take out a billboard about it. Just let one true thing come to light. See how it feels to be recognized for what's real. Mask off. Coffin open.

. . .

7. EXPRESSION & CREATIVITY

Your story might reveal this need if:

- The buried thing was creative: old writing, art, music, or abandoned work
- Your character buried something they created because it felt too vulnerable
- The uncovering brings shame, pride, or the urge to create again
- There was a silencing that led to the burial, a voice that got suppressed
- The buried thing is a story that wanted to be told, but wasn't
- Your character finally has to face what they made, what they wrote, or what they said
- Expression was buried, and now it's clawed its way to the surface

Getting to the root: What creative parts of yourself have you buried? What have you made that you hid because you weren't ready for it to be seen?

Is there an old voice, an old project, or an old self that's been waiting underground?

Real-world cultivation: Dig up one abandoned creative thing this week. Not to finish it, just to look at it. Read that first draft of your work in progress. Find the half-finished painting. Listen to the forgotten recording. Let that version of you know they're not forgotten. See if they have anything left to say. Mix it with the you now and see what comes to the surface.

8. PURPOSE & CONTRIBUTION

Your story might reveal this need if:

- The buried thing was something meant to serve others but never completed
- Your character hid a calling, a mission, or a responsibility

- The uncovering confronts them with what they failed to do, or could still do
- There was guilt about abandoning something meaningful
- The buried thing was an obligation they couldn't carry, or a gift they never gave
- Purpose was deferred, and now it's resurfacing
- What's unearthed asks: why didn't you finish what you started?

Getting to the root: What purpose have you buried? What calling have you covered over with dirt and time?

Is it still alive under there, scratching at the coffin lid? Does it still want something from you?

Real-world cultivation: If there's a buried purpose stirring, take one small step toward it this week. Not the whole excavation. Just one shovelful. Make one call. Write one paragraph. Plant one seed. See if the purpose responds. See if it's ready to come back to life.

9. GROWTH & TRANSFORMATION

Your story might reveal this need if:

- The buried thing was a past version of your character they've outgrown
- Unearthing it shows how far they've come, or confronts them with who they used to be
- There was growth in the burying, and now the growth is tested
- Your character must integrate their past self with who they are now
- The buried thing represents a chapter they closed, but maybe didn't complete
- Transformation has happened, and now the proof is surfacing
- Growth means facing what was buried, not running from it again

Getting to the root: What past version of yourself have you buried?

Have you truly integrated that self, or just hidden them under a trench-coat and fedora?

Transformation isn't about erasing who you were. It's about acknowledging your former self's strength in getting you this far, forgiving yourself, and understanding that you did the best you could with the knowledge and information you had at the time. Can you look at your buried self with love and kindness?

R**eal-world cultivation:** Find a photo, a journal entry, or an object from a past version of yourself. Someone you think you've outgrown or left behind. Look at them. Thank them. They got you here. The inner rings on the ever growing oak tree that is you.

WHAT YOUR STORY REVEALED

Take a moment to reflect.

The need(s) that resonated most:

What surprised me about what I wrote:

What my character wanted that I might want too:

One small thing I could do to honor this need:

STORY SEED #6: THE ONE WHO GOT AWAY

The Prompt:

Your character runs into someone they almost had a relationship with, but didn't. What happens after they notice each other?

Grab your pen, your laptop, and your writing appendage of choice. Set your timer. Ten minutes. And...you're off!

Welcome back. How's your heart? Let's discover what your story has to say.

Whether your story came from memory or imagination, the needs it reveals are real.

HARVEST GUIDE

What Sprouted?

The Almost: Who was this person? What made them an "almost"? Did your character end it, or did the other person/alien entity? Was it timing, circumstance, fear, or something else that kept them from becoming more?

The Moment: What passed between them in that moment? Recognition, longing, regret, relief, or something harder to name? Did time stretch or compress? Did the world go quiet, or get super loud?

The Body: What did your character's body do? Fight, flight, freeze, or flush? Did they smile, or melt into the floorboards? Did their hands fidget, did they dive behind a tree?

The After: Did they speak? What was said, or not said? Did your character walk away with something resolved, or a wound reopened? Did they regret how they handled it before they even got 40 paces?

THE NINE NEEDS

Read through each need below. Notice what resonates. Notice what resists. Once your needs are identified, skip to the Needs Compendium for a deeper dive.

1. SAFETY & SECURITY

Your story might reveal this need if:

- Your character's first instinct was to escape, hide, or pretend they didn't see
- The almost-connection ended because it didn't feel safe
- There was fear in the recognition, not just longing
- Your character felt exposed, caught, or vulnerable in a way they didn't consent to
- The other person represented danger, chaos, or instability
- Your character's nervous system went into overdrive: heart pounding, palms sweating, the works
- Safety was sacrificed for this almost-connection once before, and never again

Getting to the root: Notice if there is an almost-connection still activating your threat response. Some "almosts" weren't missed opportunities, they taught you something about yourself, your values, your standards, your beliefs. They may have been bullets dodged.

Is there someone from your past who still makes your body brace for impact? Your nervous system holds wisdom, pay attention to those signals.

Real-world cultivation: That gut instinct is always telling you something, and it could very well be that the person is unsafe, but there are times when the triggers come from within and have little to do with the other person. Examine what it was about the person that made you feel unsafe and ask how you might take your power back from that feeling. How you might stand up for yourself and not allow their energy to be overbearing. Let go of their ability to intimidate you. You are strong and fierce in your own right. You have teeth and claws and probably some pretty biting words when you want to. ;)

Trust your body's memory. If someone from your past makes you feel unsafe, even in imagination, you don't have to romanticize what didn't work just because you understand who is really in control of your fate. Some almosts stayed almost for very good reasons. Honor the part of you that walked away. They weren't on your path, make way for what comes next. And maybe it's you. ;)

2. AUTONOMY & FREEDOM

Your story might reveal this need if:

- Your character felt the pull of an old dynamic they fought hard to escape
- The almost-connection represented a version of themselves they've outgrown
- There was resentment at being thrown back into old feelings against their will
- Your character wanted to prove they'd moved on, evolved, become free
- The other person represented a cage, however gilded or pretty
- Your character felt their hard-won independence threatened

- Freedom was what they chose instead of love, and they stand by it

Getting to the root: Did you choose freedom over this person? Do you still choose it?

Notice if there's pride in your character's escape, or bittersweet grief, or both woven together like a beautiful inkblot tapestry. Maybe the cost of staying was just too high, too stifling to your soul growth.

Real-world cultivation: You're allowed to have chosen yourself. That's not selfishness. That's sovereignty. Some people walk beside us for a chapter, not the whole book. Some paths veer off for a while and may come back years later when both people/alien entities have different perspectives to share. Taking divergent paths doesn't have to mean anything bad about either of you. Hold space for infinite possibilities and rock on.

3. CONNECTION & BELONGING

Your story might reveal this need if:

- Your character ached to close the distance, to speak, or to reconnect
- The almost-connection felt like unfinished business, a story without an ending
- There was longing in your character's body, a pull toward belonging with this specific person
- Your character wondered if they'd been thought of, missed, or remembered
- The moment felt like both a lifetime and not nearly enough
- Loneliness colored the encounter, a reminder of what almost was
- Your character wanted to be known again by someone who knew them once upon a December

Getting to the root: What are you still reaching for in this almost-connection? Is it them specifically, or something they represented: being chosen, being known, being wanted? If this story came from imagination rather than memory, what does your character's longing reveal about what YOU might be seeking in connection generally?

And here's something worth a good long ponder: are you looking for belonging outside yourself because you haven't wrapped your arms around yourself fully yet? What if you belonged to yourself so completely that an almost-connection became a pleasant memory, grateful for what it was or wasn't at that time, but happy and whole and complete within yourself now. What if you were the person who chose you, missed you, and... remembered you? ;)

Real-world cultivation: If you carry an almost-connection with you, what need might they represent? What great thing do you see in them, that may be a reflection of something you can cultivate within yourself? Can you give yourself this thing, or become it? The goal isn't to stop feeling. It's to start feeling fiercely for yourself, seeing your own value unapologetically and stopping outsourcing your wholeness to others. Be here, now, in this moment with you. Be your own reunion. <3

4. UNDERSTANDING & CLARITY

Your story might reveal this need if:

- Your character wanted to know WHY it didn't work out
- The moment was spent searching the other person's face for answers
- There was a burning need to finally understand what happened
- Your character rehearsed questions they never got to ask
- The almost-connection ended in confusion, and that confusion still lingers like fog
- Your character needed this encounter to make sense of the past
- Understanding felt more important than reconnection

Getting to the root: Whether this story came from your life or your imagination, what about it still lingers? A puzzle unanswered? What question would you ask someone if you could? And why won't you?

Would their answer actually help? Would it unravel more than it resolves? Or have you been waiting for clarity that you can give yourself? Your story is your story and your point of view can be enough for a good ending.

Real-world cultivation: Some closure has to come from inside. This week, try writing the explanation you never got. From your point of view and with grace for both of you. Perhaps it was for the best and it doesn't have to mean anything is wrong with either of you or that it was the wrong choice. Can you love it for what it is/was, and let it go, knowing you may never know their point of view but that doesn't change your experience. This was as far as it went and that is okay.

5. REST & PEACE

Your story might reveal this need if:

- Your character was exhausted by the encounter, by the feelings it evoked
- The almost-connection represented drama, intensity, and upheaval they no longer have energy for
- Your character wanted the moment to be over so they could return to peace
- There was a sense of "I can't do this again, I don't have it in me"
- Peace with the past was more important than reigniting anything
- Your character has worked hard for stability and this threatens it
- The moment disrupted their bonsai tree of calm that they've carefully, and painstakingly cultivated

Getting to the root: How much of your peace have you had to build with your own two hands? Brick by brick, boundary by boundary? How protective are you of that peace now?

Does your almost-connection represent a kind of chaos you've moved away from?

Real-world cultivation: Protect your peace. Let that be your forever mantra and the filter you put the world through. If old loves, old patterns, or old intensities come knocking, you're allowed to not answer. You've earned your calm, pruned your bonsai tree. Guard it. Water it. Rest in the garden you've built and if you haven't built one yet, start now. Take a bath with the door locked, find a peaceful park, or yoga studio, or spa to zen in. Take five deep calming breaths and claim the relaxation around you.

Pay no mind to the drama behind the curtain.

6. RECOGNITION & SIGNIFICANCE

Your story might reveal this need if:

- Your character wanted to be seen as changed, evolved, better than before
- There was a desire for the almost-connection to notice, and realize what they missed
- Your character dressed for this imaginary encounter, even subconsciously
- The moment was about being witnessed, recognized, or remembered
- Your character wanted proof that they mattered to this person
- There was grief if the other person seemed unaffected, or satisfaction if they seemed shaken
- Significance in their eyes felt like validation of everything since

Getting to the root: Whose recognition are you still seeking from your past? Or, if this was pure fiction, whose recognition does your character seek, and what might that mirror in you? What would it mean if they saw you now and were impressed? What would it mean if they weren't?

Can you recognize yourself, fully and proudly, without needing them to see you? Your growth happened whether or not they noticed. It's real even if they never see it. What if your own eyes were the ones that mattered? Hmmm?

Real-world cultivation: Your growth doesn't require their applause, their gasp, their "Holy Hell you look amazing." Those things are nice, but how can you recognize yourself today? List three ways you've evolved since, or perhaps because of, that almost-connection. Let that be enough. Its own beautiful reward. Be your own ticker-tape parade.

7. EXPRESSION & CREATIVITY

Your story might reveal this need if:

- Your character had so much to say and the moment wasn't enough
- The encounter sparked a need to write, create, or process through art
- There were words trapped in your character's throat, a whole speech unsaid
- Your character expressed themselves differently when they were with this person
- The almost-connection was connected to a creative time in their life
- The story became particularly vivid, poetic, or intense as you wrote it (I'd love to witness what emerged, if you're ever willing to share at rose-raven.com <3)
- Your character felt the need to document, to capture, to make meaning from the moment

Getting to the root: What did this almost-connection unlock in you creatively? What voice did you have with them that you might have lost since?

Is there something you still need to express about this connection? Not to them, necessarily. Just... get it out? Into a journal, a song, a scream into your pillow? It's tough. It can take it!

Real-world cultivation: Write the letter you never sent. The poem they inspired. The story of what almost was. You don't have to share it with anyone. Just let it out, so you can release the burden of it. Some almost-connections become muses even in their absence. Some become far larger than they ever were in life. Have fun with it. Make lemonade from the what ifs. Make them your what ifs. <3

. . .

8. PURPOSE & CONTRIBUTION

Your story might reveal this need if:

- Your character wondered if they were meant to end up with this person
- The almost-connection represented a different path, a different life, or a different purpose
- There was a sense of cosmic significance in the encounter
- Your character questioned their choices, their current life, or their direction
- The almost-connection brought up questions of fate, destiny, or roads not taken
- Your character felt they were supposed to give something to this person that they never did
- The moment felt like a fork in the road

Getting to the root: Are you using this almost-connection to question your current path? Are they a genuine missed connection, or a way to avoid facing something about your present?

What if this encounter isn't about them at all? What if it's about you, and where you're going, and whether you're actually headed toward your own purpose? Even fictional crossroads reveal real questions about direction. Maybe they're the NPC in YOUR story. Plot twist!

Real-world cultivation: Redirect the energy. Whatever the almost-connection frothed up in you, see where you can live in purpose NOW, in your own unique way. Don't let the encounter derail you. Let it fuel you. Convert nostalgia into forward momentum.

9. GROWTH & TRANSFORMATION

Your story might reveal this need if:

- Your character saw how much they've changed since this almost-connection
- The encounter was a mirror, reflecting who they used to be

- There was pride in the distance traveled, the person they've become
- Your character barely recognized the self who loved this person
- The moment confirmed the transformation, they're not who they were
- There was grief for innocence lost, but also gratitude for growth
- Your character could finally see the relationship clearly in the rearview

Getting to the root: Let yourself feel the distance between who you were with them and who you are now.

What did this almost-connection teach you? Who did you become because it didn't work out? Is there a blessing in there? A strength, a love, a wholeness you hold because of it?

Real-world cultivation: Thank your almost-connection, even silently, in your own heart. Not for what they gave you, but for what their presence sparked in you. You didn't lose them, you found more of yourself. And that's not a tragedy, that's transformation.

If this almost-connection was fictional, thank the part of you that wrote them. Your imagination chose this story for a reason. What does it know about your growth that you haven't said out loud yet?

WHAT YOUR STORY REVEALED

Take a moment to reflect.

The need(s) that resonated most:

What surprised me about what I wrote:

What my character wanted that I might want too:

One small thing I could do to honor this need:

WHEN NOTHING RESONATES

REASONS THE PROMPTS MAY NOT HAVE LANDED (AND WHAT TO DO).

You did the prompt. You read through the nine needs. None of them landed.

That's okay, I've got you covered.

Possibility One: You're Actually Fine

Maybe you don't have pressing unmet needs right now. Huzzah! Celebrate that! Use the story seed as a prompt or character exercise and go on your merry way. Not everything has to be a Jungian excavation. Enjoy your life, and write on! :)

Possibility Two: You're Defended

Sometimes when nothing resonates, it's because everything resonates and that's too much. The defenses go up. "Nope, not me, no Ma'am. No." If you feel a little TOO dismissive, a little TOO certain that this is all a bunch of hoodoo witchcraftery… that might be worth a little look in the mirror. Check between your teeth. You might have some parsley there.

Possibility Three: The Need is Hiding

Some needs are sneaky little SOBs. They hide behind other needs. They disguise themselves with mustaches and curly red wigs. Safety might show up looking like Control. Connection might dress as People-Pleasing. Rest might masquerade as Laziness (It's not, trust me, I'm Yin certified). Give it time. Do more prompts. Take a Yin yoga class. The truth will surface when it's ready.

Possibility Four: This Isn't Your Tool

And that's okay! No one modality can be all things to all people. If this approach isn't resonating after you gave it a good go, honor that. There are many paths up the mountain...maybe even a ski-lift. Keep looking up, you are on the right track and you're worth it. <3

STANDING ON THE SHOULDERS OF GIANTS

THE HAPLESS SOULS WHOSE WORK SHAPED THIS GRIMOIRE.

This Grimoire didn't sprout from thin air. I gathered these needs from brilliant thinkers who mapped the terrain before me. If you want to go deeper into any of the nine needs, these are the roots worth exploring:

Abraham Maslow

Hierarchy of Needs

The grandfather of needs-based psychology. His pyramid (safety, belonging, esteem, self-actualization) is the foundation under everything here.

Start with: Toward a Psychology of Being

*Best for: When **Safety**, **Connection**, or **Recognition** keep surfacing and you want to see the architecture underneath all of it.*

Marshall Rosenberg

Nonviolent Communication

Taught me that every feeling points to a need, and that needs are universal. His work transformed how I understand what's underneath our emotions.

Start with: Nonviolent Communication: A Language of Life

Visit: cnvc.org

*Best for: When **Connection** or **Expression** are loud, especially if you're carrying unspoken things or struggling to ask for what you need without apology.*

Carl Jung

The Unconscious & Archetypes

Showed us that our characters, dreams, and stories are fragments of ourselves seeking integration. The shadow work underneath all of this. He was also a practicing astrologer to great effect, and his archetypes are based on the planets.

Start with: Man and His Symbols (most accessible entry point)

Best for: When ***Understanding, Growth,*** *or* ***Expression*** *are calling, and you're ready to meet the parts of yourself you've been avoiding.*

Joseph Campbell

The Hero's Journey

Revealed that story structure mirrors transformation. Every prompt here is a door on the hero's path. You are the hero in your own story. :)

Start with: The Hero with a Thousand Faces

Best for: When ***Purpose*** *or* ***Growth*** *keep showing up and you suspect there's a larger arc you're missing.*

Clarissa Pinkola Estés

Story as Medicine

Reminds us that fairy tales and myths carry soul-healing wisdom. The wild self speaks through story.

Start with: Women Who Run With the Wolves

Best for: When ***Autonomy, Expression,*** *or* ***Growth*** *are pulling at you, especially if you've been domesticated out of your own wildness.*

Brené Brown

Vulnerability & Belonging

Made it okay to talk about shame, worthiness, and the courage to be seen. Essential reading for Connection & Recognition.

Start with: The Gifts of Imperfection or Daring Greatly

Watch: TED Talk "The Power of Vulnerability"

Best for: When ***Connection, Recognition,*** *or* ***Belonging*** *ache, and you've been hiding parts of yourself to feel safe.*

Teal Swan

Shadow Work & Emotional Alchemy

Her work on parts integration, emotional processing, and meeting your own needs transformed how I understand what we bury and why. And she is HAUNTINGLY beautiful to witness. Inside and out.

Visit: tealswan.com

Watch: YouTube channel Teal Swan

*Best for: When **Safety**, **Understanding**, or **Growth** keep getting tangled up in old wounds, and you need someone unflinching to walk into the dark with you.*

Thais Gibson

Attachment Theory & Personal Development

Founder of the Personal Development School. Her work on attachment styles and subconscious reprogramming helped me understand why we reach for certain needs and push others away.

Visit: personaldevelopmentschool.com

Watch: YouTube channel Personal Development School

*Best for: When **Connection**, **Safety**, or **Autonomy** keep playing out in patterns you can't seem to break, especially in relationships.*

Edward Deci & Richard Ryan

Self-Determination Theory

The research backbone for Autonomy, Competence, and Connection as core human drives. Academic but worth it if you want the science. I am equal parts scientist and soul-surgeon.

*Best for: When **Autonomy** or **Purpose** are alive, and you want the peer-reviewed proof that what you're feeling is real, measurable, and human. It's neat. :)*

Resources for the Curious

The Gaslit Truth Podcast – Hosted by Dr. Teralyn and Therapist Jenn, this podcast spills the raw, honest tea on mental health, mopping up outdated narratives, and helping listeners navigate the labyrinthian world of therapy and psychiatric medications. If this Grimoire surfaced something that needs more than writing prompts, their work is a brilliant companion. www.thegaslittruthpodcast.com

To all of you giants: Thank You.

DID THIS HELP?

AN INVITATION TO SHARE WHAT BLOOMED.

I'd love to hear from you.

Did a prompt from here lead to a revelation for you? Or spark a new character?

Drop me a note at www.rose-raven.com or find me on Substack. Let me know if this little Grimoire made a difference.

Your feedback will help me make the next one even better. And hearing that this work landed as intended is the fuel that keeps my soul singing.

ABOUT THE AUTHOR

LILY ROSE

Astrologer. Writer. Yoga Instructor.
Professional Kaleidoscope.

Hey, you made it! And now you're wondering what Fae-type creature designed this labyrinth?

Well, I won't give you my true name, but I am a mother to an unapologetically creative Eldritch horror. I take her hiking along the bluffs of Lake Michigan and we design absurdist games with the Unreal Engine. I'm an AuDHD unicorn who's still waiting for my mothership to arrive. I called it through ET on the Atari 2600 in 1985. That's okay though. I'm patient. Infinitely patient.

Anyway, for over a decade, I've helped people weave a tapestry from their tangled balls of yarn, as a transformational astrologer, a published author across multiple books, anthologies, and magazines, and through editing for novice and Bram Stoker Award winners alike. You are all

To **Dr. Teralyn Sell**, who gave me space, grace, and her open mind, which allowed me to bridge psychology and astrology in real time. This is a foundational framework underlying everything in this book. Shhhhh.

To **Dr. Laura Motel**, my Fairy Godmother, who guided me to slow down and couple my body with my mind and soul so elegantly...and without taking any of it too seriously.

To every game master, fellow player, writing group member, editor, and storyteller who ever helped me realize that the characters we create are always telling on us in some beautiful way or another...thank you.

And to you, dear and constant reader, for trusting me with your stories and, by extension, your soul.

I solemnly swear I am up to the best kind of mischief.

Looking For Cozy Fantasy
With A Difference?
NOW ON AUDIO
SIMON MAVERICK
MAGIC, MAPS AND MISCHIEF
A COZY NEURODIVERGENT ADVENTURE
DAVID GREEN
Own Voice Autistic Fantasy
Out Now

Verbosity
More Than A Bookstore
A PLACE TO SETTLE IN AND STAY A WHILE.
123 N. FRANKLIN ST.
PORT WASHINGTON, WI 53074

MAKE ART
NOT ARSON
We bring together purpose-driven authors
to create in community
so that we can make art, not arson.
AUTHORTUNITIES
authortunities.substack.com

Breathe in peace...
...breathe out the urge to flip someone off
PORT WASHINGTON
YOGA
Tranquility in Practice
www.portwashingtonyoga.com

Printed in Dunstable, United Kingdom

91230875R00061